How to be the

BEST
BOSS
EVER

5 Steps to Rapidly Develop Yourself Into
the Leader Everyone Wants to Follow

DON FRERICKS

Inspired Press Publisher
1333 Chelsea Court
Morrow, OH 45152
www.inspiredpresspublisher.com
513-256-1792

ISBN: **978-1-7336423-1-6**

Library of Congress Control Number: 2019934681

Table of Contents

Foreword

January 2, 2019, I started my second career. After 40 years of leading financial institutions, and facing retirement, I did something out of the ordinary. Most of my career was at US Bancorp. I had the fortunate experience of being President & CEO and the Executive Chairman. I thoroughly enjoyed the many good friends that I made during my time there.

I have always been inspired by the remarkable work of Make-A-Wish and the organization's ability to fulfill wishes for children undergoing treatment for critical illnesses. Naturally, I was intrigued when Make-a-Wish asked me to consider becoming their CEO. I had never run a nonprofit before – why would they ask me?

The remarkable staff and volunteers grant a wish every 34 minutes of each day. How could I show them what to do?

After talking to the great people at Make-A-Wish, my concern that I didn't have the experience to run an international non-profit quickly diminished. What I discovered was the Make-a-Wish board didn't ask me to join them because of my nonprofit experience. They asked me to lead the organization. They wanted me for my leadership ability; and for that, I am forever grateful and humbled.

Contrary to popular opinion, I do not believe that everyone can be a leader. I believe that those who are called to lead have leadership traits deeply implanted in them early in life. Those leadership traits need to be ignited through other leaders, life experiences, and intentional development.

Three things help me determine if someone would be a good leader: their Curiosity Quotient (CQ), Emotional Intelligence (EQ), and

Intelligence (IQ), in that order. The leader with CQ 'Asks,' the leader with EQ 'Listens,' and the leader with a strong IQ 'Talks.' My banking IQ made me a good banker, but it was my CQ and EQ that made me a good leader. All three can be developed.

This book was written to help leaders and organizations learn how to improve their leadership effectiveness. *Best Boss Ever* is a book about becoming an extraordinary leader through a development process.

Don Frericks is trying to change the world, one leader at a time. I admire his effort. I have known him for 25 years, and he has always been outwardly focused and willing to do whatever it takes. His specialty is leadership development, and his unique approach of Rapid Leadership Development is helping his clients develop their best people into outstanding leaders. I admire him for his work and focus. He's right; the world desperately needs more effective leaders, and outstanding leaders make a huge difference.

He is the consummate professional who has done all things related to leadership. This book is a compilation of his continuous pursuit to find a way to develop extraordinary leaders. As a leadership development expert, Don's approach brings together best practices from across different industries.

What you will learn in this book is Don's 5-step process to become a better leader. The book will clearly lay out the steps in the process one should go through to improve their leadership effectiveness. Don has selflessly laid out his proprietary process, from which everyone can benefit. What I like the most about his book is that he doesn't sugar coat anything. Leadership development is hard work because changing our behavior is hard work. This book is not for the faint of heart. It is written for those who want to go for it and develop their skills as rapidly as possible.

Don's coaching style is inspirational, and this book will provide you with the know-how and motivation that you need to become an extraordinary leader. *Best Boss Ever* will show you how to do strength development in ways you may have never imagined. It will also give you the insights you need to practice and "deeply reflect" on what you are learning from your leadership practice. ***Best Boss Ever*** will help you overcome the obstacles to developing your skills until they become habits.

Four out of five people fail to develop themselves into an extraordinary leader; but armed with the process that is detailed in this book, you can flip the odds around. Everything you need is in this easy-to-read book. I hope you will take it seriously and implement everything Don lays out for you.

Now that I have started my second career, I am going to focus on how I can best use my leadership ability. More importantly, I will work to serve my people and the organization in extraordinary ways. I want to be remembered as one of those people who others talk about a year later as their "***Best Boss Ever.***"

Richard K. Davis
Chief Executive Officer of the Make-A-Wish Foundation

Introduction

"Good is the enemy of excellence. Leadership is the challenge to be something more than average."

Jim Rohn[1]

There are three types of people who manage others:

1. Those who make others' lives miserable
2. Those who are good enough that no one complains about them
3. Those who inspire us to be the best we can be

For how many poor leaders have you worked? Did they make your life miserable? Many of these people have no idea what they are doing to lead others, and they suffer from blind spots concerning the difference between management and leadership. By and large, they are technically proficient and are not trying to be a terrible leader. Unfortunately, they create a culture that enables, or even facilitates, disengagement, low productivity, and high turnover.

Average leaders, on the other hand, don't create disengagement, low productivity and high turnover. But they also don't lead their teams through conflicts, complex problem solving, and important decisions in a way that creates high engagement. It's hard to lead in a way that inspires and motivates others. These people are not considered bad leaders; they just don't bring out the best in their people. Subsequently, their team is average at best.

Because poor leaders have such a negative impact, we think average leaders are good enough. Maybe you have thought this yourself. But, it's not good enough in today's business environment. Whenever better is possible, why settle for 'average?'

Leadership has a deep and dramatic effect on the way employees deliver the company's products and services. Remember, the customer's experience is in the hands of your employees. On average, two-thirds of American workers are disengaged. Though leadership may not be the only reason for disengagement, it is widely identified as the leading cause.

Great leaders are authentic and genuine. They lead individuals to be the best version of themselves, and they create high performing teams that accomplish amazing results. It seems that great leaders have common characteristics. However, they also have dramatically different personality traits, preferences, skills, and knowledge. Outstanding leadership can be accomplished in many ways, but it has some well-defined characteristics. The good news is, you don't have to be perfect, and you don't have to be skilled in all leadership areas, to be considered an outstanding leader.

Being an outstanding leader and creating high performing teams feels good, and it is the main reason we chose to be in leadership positions. To experience success as a leader is to know your leadership matters to your team, and that it makes a difference in your business' results.

Jack Zenger and Joe Folkman studied over 20,000 leaders and documented their findings in their book, *The Extraordinary Leader*.[2] Their findings show the impact of incredible leaders:

- The top-tenth percentile leaders had almost <u>double</u> the amount of customer satisfaction than the bottom leaders.
- Great leaders generated <u>more than twice</u> as much net income as the good leaders.
- Sales leaders in the top decile of leadership effectiveness had sales teams that generated <u>more than six times</u> the amount of sales than bottom decile leaders.
- The highest rated leaders had over four times the employees "willing to go the extra mile" than the poor leaders.

This book will describe the process of how to become an outstanding leader and give you the best practices of those who have already achieved leadership success. Imagine now what it would be like to hear someone tell their friend that working for you was the best part of their entire career. That YOU were by far the BEST BOSS they EVER worked for!

If you have never attempted to improve your leadership skills, you might wonder if it is possible to become an outstanding leader. It's hard work; but my experience suggests that anyone with enough motivation can become outstanding. Tony's story will give you an example of the challenge and opportunity presented by developing your leadership. Put yourself in Tony's shoes - imagine what it would be like to experience his challenges and eventually overcome them.

Tony's Story

Tony was a middle-aged professional who loved his company and desperately wanted to grow his career. He had no problem with taking on more responsibility, and would work extremely hard to do whatever it took to be successful. People described him as a 'good guy,' without any 'red flags,' but not especially great at leading others. Tony was recently promoted to vice-president of his company.

As a 'driver,' he spent more time at work than most of his team. His work ethic and drive for accomplishment were his strengths. However, in this new position, working hard wasn't enough. He thought if everyone on his team would work as hard as he did, things would get better.

His team felt his judgment. They could sense his loss of confidence in their abilities. The workload increased. The team brought all their problems to Tony because they didn't want to make a mistake. Most of his team experienced loads of stress and frustration. Tony began to notice the problem with his team, but it wasn't until his wife pointed out to him that something needed to change that he realized he was in over his head.

After innumerable sleepless nights, Tony resolved to do something about his situation. His boss had previously worked with a coach. Tony wondered if he were to meet with someone outside of the company, if they could help him see what was going on. When he met with the coach, she suggested to begin by getting feedback about his leadership effectiveness. Tony did, and the results revealed that he had a blind spot: he was uninspiring and somewhat de-motivating; moreover, he was also perceived to be chiefly interested in himself and untrustworthy.

xii   Best Boss Ever

Tony improved several leadership actions. He chose to 'practice' inspiring and motivating others to high performance. He learned to build trust and respect through an emotional connection. And to do that, he had to lessen his focus on driving results and practice better communication with his people. Over time, he learned to let go and get out of his team's way. As a result, his team became more engaged and productive, thereby increasing their results.

Tony's success began when he created a development plan and integrated that plan into his calendar while focusing on creating new habits. Tony knew that his leadership ability must be developed; intellectually learning about leadership would only make him smarter.

Throughout the process, Tony's coach helped him learn about himself and increase his self-awareness. He learned things about himself that he hadn't noticed before, and discovered why he did those things. To improve our leadership, we often need to fully understand why we do what we do.

There is much more to the journey Tony went through, but at the heart of it was a simple process of:

1. Choosing the most leverageable leadership competency to work on
2. Creating a robust plan of action
3. Tracking progress
4. Anticipating & removing obstacles
5. Seeking ongoing feedback

Before we learn the process that will transform you into an outstanding leader, let's explore why outstanding leadership matters. Tony started with a strong motivation to improve his leadership effectiveness because he had a burning platform. Leaders who are driven to improve will experience success in creating new habits, if they follow the process. Becoming the BEST BOSS EVER is in sight, if you have a big motivation!

Chapter One

Why Outstanding Leadership Matters

"The quality of leadership, more than any other single factor, determines the success or failure of an organization."

Fred Fiedler and Martin Chemers[3]

Can leadership effectiveness improve an organization? Does outstanding leadership have an impact on business results?

Reflect on a time when you worked for a poor leader or bad boss. Did you do your best work? Did you feel engaged, satisfied, motivated, or inspired? Were you willing to go the extra mile? Take risks? Be creative and offer innovative solutions?

How did it feel? Did you feel good about the company and the work you accomplished, or was that overshadowed by the dissonance between you and your boss? Think of your emotional and mental energy — how much was being wasted? Were you understood and fully heard? Did you feel valued and trusted?

When trust is violated and you feel disrespected, it becomes a huge de-motivator and performance suffers. I personally have experienced the black cloud of discouragement following me and reminding me of how much I hated my job. It eats away at you.

Joe was a Great Boss

But I have also lived on the flipside. My corporate career started in Cincinnati at a company that was rapidly growing and had a very successful brand. I was hired by 'Joe,' the number three executive in the company at the time. He was one of the most professional people I have ever met. Because of the way he carried himself, you immediately thought he was a first-class individual. He had style and exuded confidence. He placed a large amount of trust in me when I had no background in the industry. I felt respected by him because he demonstrated his confidence in me by letting me determine how to meet my objectives. He was always available.

Joe requested to have some oversight about what I was doing, but never made me think I didn't have some autonomy. That approach motivated me a to go the extra mile — a feeling that I only have when I feel trusted and respected to determine the best way to accomplish the goals and objectives I have been given.

Joe was a wonderful guide and possessed a tremendous amount of knowledge about the industry and the company. However, I never felt "not smart enough" around his tremendous experience. He knew how to insert his knowledge in a way that was useful, but didn't make me feel stupid.

Joe kept track of my travels; the branches where I worked and the reps on whom I made sales calls. More importantly, he knew the branches where I was making progress. Joe made it clear to me that he was more interested in the impact I was having on those branches instead of my travel schedule. I knew we were on the same page, and his support to help me improve sales encouraged me to travel 75% of my time.

When I ran into obstacles, such as a GM not buying into my program, Joe would have a conversation with them to make sure they 'got it.' He made his expectations clear to his GMs; even though they did not report to me, they were clear that I had Joe's support to do what I was doing. Joe would not tolerate their reps not going on sales calls with me or preventing the sales training from happening.

With his support and leadership, I increased sales productivity in all but one branch. My success came from hard work; but I could not have done it without Joe's support and direction. I enjoyed working for him a great deal, and as a result, I invested an extraordinary effort into my job. I was successful, and his leadership made a positive impact on my performance.

Average or Less is the Norm

No wonder only one-third of American workers are engaged; most workers are upset and disappointed in the boss. Often, we blame the employee for not doing their best, so many of them give up. These employees are only looking to do the minimum required to do their job. They are often described as:

- Lacking positive energy and engagement
- Not communicating well with others
- Not trying to collaborate
- Not taking the initiative to solve problems
- Getting easily triggered and defensive

Most people come to work wanting to do a good job. But a large majority become disengaged due to poor leadership. There are many ways to lead poorly. How many times have you heard people complain about a manager who doesn't manage "fairly?" That manager seems to have favorites and everyone else on the team doesn't matter. I have also heard employees become extremely frustrated by the manager who doesn't know the work processes and doesn't try to understand the employees' process challenges. A classic complaint about a poor boss is that they are never available or rarely talk to the employees.

Infrequent communication and poor relationships make employees feel like their boss just doesn't care about them. People don't care about how much you know until they know how much you care.

Employees become disengaged for many reasons, but the bosses who are poor leaders have the biggest impact on engagement. People don't usually quit their company, they quit working for a boss they don't trust and respect.

The best employees will have other employment options; and the employees who don't feel they have any other option will stay. These are the employees who have "quit and stayed." They physically come to work, but are not emotionally or mentally engaged. They will not change or become more effective unless leaders encourage them to change.

In the United States, research shows two-thirds of our employees are disengaged. Gallup estimates that actively disengaged employees cost the U.S. $483 billion to $605 billion each year in lost productivity.[4] Billions of dollars of productivity lost due to employees who don't feel connected to their organization.

It's not hard to understand that poor leaders don't bring out the best in people. The more important question is: How much of a difference does a great leader make? Or, what is the impact of outstanding leadership?

Great leaders create high levels of trust with their team. Trust earns a leader relationship capital, which enables them to have influence. With influence, they can empower, engage, and enroll team members. Great leaders inspire and motivate others and their teams to perform at a high level. Like in my personal story about Joe, great leaders make you willing to go the extra mile. People who are following an outstanding leader are more satisfied, more productive, and more creative. Great leadership enables employees to consistently act this way. High levels of employee engagement and employee retention are only possible with outstanding leadership.

Effective leadership does not solve all of our problems, but it goes a long way to engage our people in solving business problems and challenges. Much has been written about the Millennial generation. It seems this generation has less tolerance for many things. They may have less patience for lack of a career plan or not being trained, but most importantly, they seem to not tolerate bad leadership.

I asked outstanding leaders about the worst boss they ever had. One lady remembered vividly the overwhelming negative impact that a poor leader had on her. As she told me the story, she came to tears recalling how demeaning and difficult the poor leader acted toward her. Nothing she did was recognized as positive, and she was continually reminded why she was "never good enough." It affected her so deeply that she almost quit. The boss' behavior made her miserable and stressed her out, and her performance suffered.

Leaders are not totally responsible for their employees' engagement, but they do strongly influence their employees. Great leaders help employees see, feel, and care about the things that will keep them engaged.

I like to focus on "neutral" (not fully engaged or actively disengaged) employees. They can be swayed on any given day to be engaged or disengaged. If you are an outstanding leader, you can influence the neutral employees to join the 33% who are already engaged. If you are a poor leader, you give the neutral employee reasons to be disengaged. Employees come to a new job hoping to work for a boss who will treat them with respect and help them enjoy their work. Poor leaders enable the negative employees to influence their peers with their negativity. It's a big problem when the most vocal and disengaged employees are influencing your other employees to be disengaged. Your leadership matters!

If you only get one thing out of this book, realize that your leadership effectiveness has a direct impact on employee engagement, and employee engagement has a direct impact on your company's bottom line.

When you lead in an outstanding way, your employees become more engaged. Employees who have a stronger emotional connection to your business are more likely to go the extra mile and be creative. Innovation comes from engaged employees. You need more engaged employees!

Reflection Questions

At the end of each chapter, I'll include some thought-provoking questions that you can use to think about how the chapter's ideas affect you and your leadership.

- How much better could your team perform?
- What would happen if their engagement level increased?
- Imagine your employees telling you how much they enjoy working for you and that you have made a difference in their life. What would you be willing to do to achieve that?
- If you could increase your team's fulfillment, purpose, and passion, how much effort and time would you invest to learn how to do that?

Chapter Two

Are Outstanding Leaders
Made or Born?

*"Leaders are made, they are not born. They are made by hard
effort, which is the price all of us must pay to achieve any
goal that is worthwhile."*

Vince Lombardi[5]

Before we move on, there is one more thing that you need to examine
and believe before you are ready to launch into rapidly developing
your leadership skills. Our beliefs determine our actions. They are powerful causes for what we do and what we don't do.

Does "A + B = C"?

Your attitudes always precede your behaviors. Few actions, if ever, are
completely random. What you do is based on what you think. It is almost
impossible to do something contrary to what you think. So, your mindset will either enable your development or minimize it. I like using the
"ABCs of development" in workshops to help people realize the power
of their thinking. In this model the A = antecedents, B = beliefs, and C =
consequential feelings.

It is common to believe that the things that happen to us create our feelings; or, A = C. When a car cuts you off on the highway in a high-speed lane change, which you didn't anticipate, you scream and become mad at the other driver, probably cursing at him or her. In this case, we say that the other driver "made me upset and angry." The reality is, the other driver did not make you feel anything. He or she was just driving. Our interpretation of this person's driving as reckless made us mad.

The real question is: Do the antecedents (A's) of our lives <u>combined with</u> the beliefs (B's) about those things equal the consequential feelings (C's)? Yes, the antecedents, or the stuff that just happens, is interpreted by our past experiences and beliefs, and, once that filter is applied, the emotional brain rapidly creates a "consequential feeling." We all "interpret" the events of our lives and make our feelings.

One of the biggest leadership challenges is leading yourself well. What this means is being aware of your reaction to the events of your life and making a choice. For example, I have caught an initial feeling, and chose not to let it turn into something else.

Following a recent close call with another driver switching lanes rapidly, I caught my initial reaction in real time. I said "Wow! That was intense and scared the hell out of me. I don't know why they are driving that way. I don't want to feel angry or upset. I'm going to breathe deeply, be peaceful, and not blame the other person for what happened. I don't know the whole story." This probably sounds weird. but it works to reduce anxiety and keep from getting unnecessarily upset.

Believe It and You Will See It

To become an outstanding leader, you need to *believe that you can become* an outstanding leader. There is no reason to start the process unless you believe you can do it. Are you holding onto any fixed mindset beliefs about your ability? "I'm not _____." Fill in the blank with your favorite reason – smart enough, charismatic, good at expressing my thoughts, trained, good with people, don't have a mentor, don't have a good team, or many more. To some, it may feel like it is almost impossible to become an outstanding leader. The antecedent in the development of a leader's effectiveness is whatever happens to them.

Those who develop themselves into great leaders get out of their comfort zones. To be uncomfortable and do the heavy lifting of development, you must believe it will be worth it. People grow into outstanding leaders when they stop using bad habits of leadership and adopt new effective habits.

For instance, if you tell yourself that even though you are not a great listener, there are many others who are worse than you, you will justify in your mind not trying to become a great listener. Before you begin this journey, you must believe that you can develop into an outstanding leader.

Do you think outstanding leaders are made or born?

If you searched for what leadership gurus believe on this topic, you would find the majority asserting that they think leaders are developed. I also validated this with an outstanding leaders study. All but one believed that leaders were for the most part, developed. They did not believe people were born leaders, because they saw others who worked for them improve their leadership skill and ability. And they experienced it firsthand. Many would say they were not that great of a leader at the beginning of their career. They told several funny stories about the terrible leadership mistakes they made; and yet, they all became outstanding over time.

Could extraordinary leaders start their career with skills, ability, or personality traits that helped them grow faster and become outstanding leaders? One person in my study suggested that social preferences may help us be perceived as an effective leader. For instance, those who have the preference for extraversion get energy just from being with people. They love being with others and that energy is felt by their team. It seems to point toward extroverts being perceived as leaders because they love being around people.

However, my experience suggests that personality traits and social styles do not *make us* leaders. There is no way that extraversion makes you a leader and introversion doesn't make you a leader. Personality and social preference are a small part of the overall equation that makes people effective leaders.

What Does It Take to Develop Yourself into an Outstanding Leader?

I was recently asked by a potential client to share the main characteristics of people who transform themselves into great leaders. I answered with four characteristics; but the most important one is the first, and the other three cannot make up for the lack of the first. The all-important first characteristic is big motivation — they have a huge reason to change. In case you are wondering about the other three characteristics of those who are successful at becoming great leaders, they are:

- Clear goals & objectives
- Grit/determination/persistence
- Reflection

The point of sharing this is, no matter how good the process to develop yourself into something you are not today, if you don't believe it can work for you, and your motivation is not red-hot, it will be extremely difficult to develop your leadership skills. There is a great deal of 'practice' required, and people stop practicing when they don't have big motivation.

Back to the initial question: Are leaders made or born? It is important for you to truthfully answer this question because, if you don't believe leaders are made, you are not setting yourself up for success in developing your leadership skills.

Outstanding leaders are developed/made, and we all start developing our skills in different places. My years of experience have given me a strong belief, because I have seen it done repeatedly. Anyone can become a better leader, and many can become outstanding leaders.

Everyone's journey is unique. We all start our process of becoming an outstanding leader in different places and with different skills and abilities. Some people may have advantages in personality or preferences or upbringing, but we can all get better, and all of us can develop extraordinary strengths. This belief is foundational for your leadership development. If you don't believe it completely, spend time investigating why not.

Develop a motivation to become a better leader, and you will not be negatively affected by the time, energy, and persistence it demands. If you don't have an enormous amount of motivation, your ability to sustain your development will be thwarted by obstacles. Distractions, loss of focus, and not having enough time will always be there to tempt you to stop working. Building new habits requires consistent effort. Consistent effort requires energy and commitment.

Are You Ready to Become an Outstanding Leader?

One of my clients is a mountain climber. He has conquered many of the most intimidating summits in the world. One of the most challenging mountains to climb is Mt. Everest. Even though my friend is an expert climber, he became injured on his first attempt to climb Everest. People have died trying to climb Everest, so it would be okay to say, "I tried, and it didn't work out." But he didn't say that to himself. He immediately started to plan and prepare to climb it the next year. If you choose to become an outstanding leader, you will need the same level of preparation, commitment, and follow-through.

Dr. Prochaska and his associates wrote a book called *Changing for Good: A Revolutionary Six-Stage Program for Overcoming Bad Habits and Moving Your Life Positively Forward.* The researchers wanted to understand why some people can change themselves (stop drinking, smoking, using drugs, lose weight, etc.). As psychologists, their businesses were established to help people make changes in their lives, and they desired to help more people.

"Fully 45 percent of people who make an appointment with a professional therapist drop out of therapy after only a few sessions. We wondered if there might be a connection between dropout rates and mismatched stages and processes. We wanted to test whether our model could predict the rate at which people would drop out of certain therapies. Our results were astonishing. Our model was 93 percent predictive of which clients would drop out."[6]

The program assumes that, although the amount of time an individual spends in a specific stage varies, everyone must accomplish the same "stage-specific tasks" to move through the process. *Efficient self-change depends on doing the right things at the right times."* [7]

The stages are **precontemplation, contemplation, preparation, action, maintenance,** and **termination.** To make a big change in your life, i.e., to become an outstanding leader, it's important to follow the stages. Here's how the stages could be applied to leadership development:

1. **Precontemplation** - You do not intend to develop your leadership skills in the next six months.

2. **Contemplation** - You intend to practice and develop effective leadership behaviors in the next six months.

3. **Preparation** - You intend to practice and develop leadership behaviors in the next 30 days.

4. **Action** - You have been effectively practicing leadership development for less than six months.

5. **Maintenance** - You have been effectively practicing leadership development for more than six months.

6. **Termination** - You are done: your problem will no longer present any temptation or threat, and your behavior will not return.

Prochaska writes: "*When we are mired in the precontemplation stage, it is denial that holds us there.*"[8]

Too often I have heard people say, "I have known for years that _____ was an issue," or "I have had that all my life," or "I was told by a couple of my past managers that this was an issue." These are statements from those who are stuck in precontemplation.

Contemplation begins when we wonder about what it would be like to be different, and how it would have an impact on ourselves and our team. If you manage people, you experience some frustration and suffering as a leader. When you deeply desire to be less frustrated and annoyed by your team, and imagine what it would be like to have less suffering, you have begun the contemplation phase.

Something often happens that awakens us, and then we think, "My suffering as a leader is not because of my people's inadequacies, but because I need to be better." This kind of insight or enhanced awareness can be a bridge from contemplation to preparation. You are not ready to develop yourself unless you are in 'contemplation.'

Are You in the Precontemplation or Contemplation Stage?

Before you picked up this book, did you ever think about becoming an extraordinary leader? At this point in the book, you have likely began contemplating if it is something you should do.

To determine if you are firmly in contemplation, think back to the past week, or past month at the longest. Rate your answer with the following scale: 1 = Never; 2 = Seldom; 3 = Occasionally; 4 = Often; and 5 = Repeatedly.

- Do you look for information related to being a better leader?
- Do you think about information from articles and books on how to overcome being a poor leader?
- Do you read about people who have become highly successful leaders?
- Do you easily recall information that people have given you about the benefits of becoming a great leader?

SCORE:

People who are in the contemplation phase usually score 10 or more.

If you score less than 10, you are probably in the precontemplation phase. Don't start putting together a plan to develop your leadership ability until you have fully contemplated why you want to be outstanding, and how you will benefit from being a great leader.

Prochaska further clarifies: "*The first step in fostering intentional change is to become conscious of the self-defeating defenses that get in our way. Knowledge is power. We must acknowledge our defenses before we can defeat or circumvent them.*"[9]

Reflection Questions

- What doubts do you have about your ability to become an outstanding leader?
- How can you suspend your doubts until you try to develop yourself?
- What's your motivation to become an outstanding leader?
- If it is a small motivator, what could you do to double your motivation?

Chapter Three

Why Leadership Development Doesn't Work

"Here's the thing – when it comes to leadership, the training industry has been broken for years. You don't train leaders, you develop them . . ."

Mike Myatt[10]

It might sound a little strange for a leadership development expert to say that leadership development programs don't work – that they don't successfully develop leaders; but there is plenty of evidence that suggests this is true.

Deloitte Insights: Leadership Awakened

"Fully 89% of executives in this year's (2016) survey rated the need to strengthen, reengineer, and improve organizational leadership as an important priority. The traditional pyramid-shaped leadership development model is simply not producing leaders fast enough to keep up with the demands of business and the pace of change.

More than half of surveyed executives (56%) report their companies are not ready to meet leadership needs. In fact, more than one in five companies

(21%) have no leadership programs at all. Our findings suggest that organizations need to raise the bar in terms of rigor, evidence, and more structured and scientific approaches to identifying, assessing, and developing leaders, and that this process needs to start earlier in leaders' careers."[11]

Mike Myatt wrote a wonderful article at Forbes.com, "*The #1 Reason Why Leadership Development Fails.*"[12] His assessment is that, even though we collectively invest billions ($50 billion) of dollars on leadership-based education, we don't have the results to show for it. Most companies do not measure the effectiveness of their leadership development programs. Even if they start their program with a baseline measurement, they don't end with a post-measurement. In addition to poor measurement, very few programs are developmental; they don't include a process to change behavior.

Myatt's solution: "Don't train leaders—coach them, mentor them, disciple them, and develop them, but please don't attempt to train them."

Unfortunately, becoming an outstanding leader is not like most things you have 'learned' to do in your life. The process is different. If you only intellectually learn about leadership, you just become smarter about leading others. Don't get me wrong, knowledge about leadership is important. Leadership is about behaviors, and to become a better leader, we usually must remove bad habits and develop more effective habits of leading others. To become an outstanding leader requires consistent practice of these habits, and reflection on what you are learning as you practice.

What's the solution? The "70-20-10 model" provides some guidance: make sure only 10% of your development process is training oriented. Twenty percent should be focused on the relationships; boss, direct reports, and your peers. Finally, a great development program puts 70% of the effort toward doing the work of leadership and practicing effective leadership actions. To do this, you will need a well-thought-out process.

Leadership Training is Popular

From my experience, it seems that most companies don't have their own leadership training programs. For sure this is true with small-to-medium-sized businesses. However, the pendulum swings the other way for medium-to-large companies – most either outsource or conduct their own training. That is why there are so many choices in the market for leadership training. An article on the Training Industry website reveals that leadership training is a $366 billion global ($166 billion in the U.S.) industry.[13]

In your career, have you been trained how to lead others? I believe most great leaders in their fifties would say that they have attended leadership training at some point in their career. And most of those people would say the training was helpful. Some may have even had a transformative experience.

However, if you ask the question, as I have, "Did this training make you a great leader?" Almost all would say they didn't become an outstanding leader because they attended leadership training. This is the crux of the problem. We treat the leadership effectiveness problem as if it were any other challenge that we have when we don't know how to do something. We allow ourselves to think that leadership training (an event) is the same as leadership development (a process). The more complex the skill set we are trying to learn, the more difficult it is to learn it solely through training.

I have been in the training industry as a consultant, trainer, and internal practitioner. I was once in charge of the training department for a large corporation, and back in the day, we did a massive amount of training. Most of our courses received high marks. I would hear many accolades about the value of the training. However, when I would follow up with people to see what they were doing differently a month after the class, their feedback was usually sobering: *"Well, I've been super busy and haven't been able to do everything I wanted to do."* In other words, they didn't implement much of what they learned, and therefore did not change their behaviors.

The companies who use a process to develop leaders are in the minority. The majority of companies who say they do leadership *development*, actually do leadership *training*. I have a wonderful client who has a nine-month program with three very good workshops. We start with a

360-degree assessment and end with a capstone project. After the initial nine months, the participants are turned loose until they are reassessed approximately nine to eleven months later with the same 360-degree assessment. It's a highly valued program by participants and their executives. Their process of leadership development is not perfect, and could be much better with coaching, but it is a great example of a process versus an event.

Sometimes a company will outsource their leadership development to a university executive program or training company. (I just received an invitation today to attend a training program at Stanford Business Executive Education for a week on various topics for $13,000.) Can you imagine your company investing that kind of money in your future? All these training programs are reported by the participant as a good experience. People always learn some things about themselves that they didn't know before, and they usually learn some interesting things about leadership. This all sounds good, right?

When Doesn't it Work?

First, leadership development doesn't work when it isn't being done. If my assessment is correct, the greatest failure of business is not developing leaders. Second, due to the immense complexity of the challenge of successfully leading people, training by itself does not work. Therefore, companies who only provide training for leaders also fail.

I realize it may seem that providing leadership training is better than nothing, but it does not mean that better leaders are being developed. If you measure success based on people's reactions to training programs, most programs would get flying colors. For instance, a large company based in Cincinnati puts some of their leaders through a four-and-a-half-day 'college' experience. Participants are given 360-degree feedback and they create leadership development plans. The week of learning is experiential and includes simulations, board games, engaging competition, and dinners with executives. It is well designed and focused on helping participants become better leaders. The college has one of the highest ratings in the company. So, it is perceived to be very successful.

Six to ten months after the college, the participants are encouraged to take the 360-degree assessment again to determine how much progress they have made at improving their leadership competencies and their overall leadership effectiveness. Unfortunately, most people don't take the assessment again. Why? I'm not sure, but some have changed assignments, some are too busy, and some are concerned that their scores will be lower because they have not been working their development plan. I think if you were working on your leadership ability and seeing progress, you would want to be assessed again.

Of those who do take the re-assessment, 56% see some progress and half of those people see tremendous progress. Does that sound like success? Out of 24 participants, 14 take the re-assessment, 7-8 get better results the second time around. That doesn't seem to be very good to me. The company I am talking about is a large global company that has been considered one of the top ten leadership development companies in the world for many years. If you were an executive in that company, would you be happy with a 25% improvement rate? Yes, if you considered success being the post-course evaluations. But that is the wrong evaluation of success.

I have seen this type of opportunity at many companies, and when I am engaged to consult with their programs and turn them into robust processes, we see significant results. If all you did was to include an accurate measurement tool at the beginning and the end of the process, you would see improvement. However, I know of very few companies that have a robust leadership development process that includes this type of measurement.

Outstanding Leaders Study

One of the best projects I have done was a qualitative study about how people became great leaders. I interviewed many outstanding leaders I have come to know over my career. All had achieved a level of senior leadership within their company. Additionally, these are the kind of people who others respect for their leadership ability. Throughout the interviewing process, I enjoyed getting to know each of these leaders for their unique qualities. They were so different, and yet there were similarities in their journeys. I documented the patterns and themes of their leadership journeys.

I became interested in their learning experiences, and, of course, many had attended a leadership workshop, listened to webinars, and read many articles and books; but only a couple suggested that leadership "training" dramatically helped them to become a better leader. Why is that? Because, as I stated before, you can't intellectually learn your way to becoming a great leader.

Each of the leaders I talked with had an organic process of development that just evolved. Their special skills were "paying attention" and "connecting the dots;" moreover, they were outstanding at observing poor leaders and great leaders and discerning the differences in their actions. They became upset with the things poor leaders did and committed to not making those mistakes. Just as important, they became inspired by great leaders, and did everything they could to emulate the things great leaders did.

I laughed with one of the participants as he told a story about how his mentor told him to stop emulating the mentor so much and learn how to lead in his own way. Copycats are not authentic, and the leaders I talked with all determined how to be authentic with their style and preferences.

How Long Will It Take?

One of the big challenges with leadership development and why it doesn't work is that it takes too long. Even with an effective process, it could last several years. But there is no way of being able to know for sure. There are numerous variables; everyone starts in a different place, and everyone's journey is different. If you are starting with many strengths, it might only take 12 – 18 months.

Leaders with blind spots often start their development process slowly because they don't embrace their feedback. Additionally, removing a bad habit takes more effort than enhancing a strength. Some of these people may need three years to grow their skills and ability.

Another factor that impacts how quickly someone develops is how much they practice. If you practice every day versus every month, you will have much faster growth. If you learn something from every practice opportunity, you will quickly learn what works and what doesn't. If you ask others for feedback about your progress, their feedback will inform you of what you can do differently to be more effective. If you don't ask for feedback, you develop slowly.

When I asked outstanding leaders how long it took them to become outstanding at leadership, most didn't know how to answer the question. Because their process was an organic development process and didn't have an action plan attached to it, they couldn't gauge how long it took. From my perspective, it seemed like it might have taken them ten or more years. We don't have that kind of time in today's business environment to wait for outstanding leaders to develop. The quicker, the better.

One of my clients was an outstanding athlete growing up and became very skilled at playing shortstop. He remembers clearly that his skill increased dramatically when he asked the coach to hit extra ground balls after every practice. He improved as he practiced deeply. This applies directly to leadership development and is actually a breakthrough. You can become an outstanding leader by learning to practice leadership and "taking extra ground balls" until your new habits are firmly in place. And the more ground balls you take, the faster you will become a great leader.

Mastery

In 2008, Malcom Gladwell published a *New York Times* bestseller called *Outliers*. His book made popular the idea that mastery takes 10,000 hours of practice (90 minutes a day for 20 years).[14]

The original research was done by Anders Ericsson, who detailed through his observations of world-class performers that mastery was less about a specific number of hours but more about a type of practice. "Deliberate practice" was making mistakes and then stopping, reflecting, and adjusting. Additionally, skills were broken down into sub-skills to be mastered one by one. For instance, rather than trying to master a tennis serve, the student would practice and master just tossing the tennis ball to the right location and height with complete accuracy.

Gladwell was trying to expose the idea that innate skill or natural ability was not the main source of excellence for those who became world renowned. His interpretation of the Ericsson research pointed toward the need to practice in a more intentional way: slowly, over and over, breaking the big task down into smaller tasks and working on small errors. I contend this is the missing ingredient in leadership development. I prefer to call this "deep practice." Those who desire to be outstanding leaders will benefit greatly from practicing deeply, thus combining evaluation and reflection about what worked and what did not.

"Life" is one of the greatest teachers, and we all need to pay more attention to our lessons. All leaders need personal mastery. Noticing how we showed up to a meeting and what our impact was, and why we behaved in the manner we did is what outstanding leaders do to remain outstanding. They don't try to be perfect, but they do try to continually learn from everything they do.

Learning Agility

Neta Moye is the faculty director of Leadership Development Programs and Clinical Professor of Management at the Owen Graduate School of Management. I love her definition of learning agility: "Learning agility is the term used to describe those best equipped to learn the most from their experiences. At its most basic level, learning agility refers to a constellation of characteristics—raw aptitudes and abilities, as well as attitudes and skills—that relate to an individual's readiness and ability to learn from experiences."[15]

Your learning agility is the engine of your leadership development. It is seen as the single best predictor of executive success, even above intelligence and education. Make sure you give it plenty of fuel by reflecting on what you are learning.

Syed's & Sharon's Story

Syed was a mid-level manager at a large consumer packaged goods company. He had been recently promoted when he received his first 360-degree assessment. His new team rated him as a good leader with one "profound" strength. He desired to become a much better leader and, over the course of 18 months, dedicated himself to regularly practicing different sub-skills of leadership. He was consistent and often took the time to think about the things he was doing and how they were working. He liked reflecting on what he was doing because it gave him insights.

Syed was persistent at practicing leadership skills in different ways. Through his practice, he gradually was perceived as a better leader, someone who was intentional about becoming better. Often, when we pick the right thing to work on, we can be perceived in a much better light. He chose well, and he was consistent. Eighteen months later, Syed was reassessed, and he found his survey results significantly improved. He had several emerging strengths, but this time, instead of just one profound strength, he had 10. Incredible improvement in 18 months!

On the other hand, here is the example of another super smart brand manager: this is the story of Sharon. She was a super-smart brand executive who focused on building the business and solving complex marketing challenges with great data and rich information about the market. Her 360-degree assessment took her by surprise because she noticed a low score in an area that was important to her team and her boss. Zenger and Folkman refer to this as a "fatal flaw,"[16] and it is fatal to one's leadership effectiveness if you don't change it. Unfortunately, when you have a fatal flaw, all others see are the things you do poorly. Unfortunately, during her development process, Sharon chose to work on other things, and her weakness continued to distract her team. When she did her reassessment, Sharon's results were not any better. She was immensely frustrated and mad that she had wasted her time not developing the right leadership skills. Don't be Sharon!

If you follow my process closely, you will see significant progress in six months, and in 12 to 18 months, good leaders become great. However, if you start the process with a fatal flaw weakness and no significant strengths, it could take up to three years of steady practice. In less time than it takes to earn a bachelor's degree, almost anyone can transform themselves into an outstanding leader. Having said that, very few people start with a defined process. No matter how persistent you are, without a great process, you won't become a great leader, unless you are willing to work at it for a long time.

The rest of this book will be dedicated to what a rapid leadership development process looks like, and how to implement it successfully. I'll break the process down into five steps and provide enough information that if you chose to do it yourself, you will have a good road map to follow.

The five steps to rapidly developing yourself as an outstanding leader are:

1. **Choose Wisely What to Improve** (Chapter 4)

    1.1   Increase Self-awareness of Your Leadership Strengths and Weaknesses.

    1.2   Who Is Your Yardstick? (Who Do You Compare Yourself Against?)

    1.3   Repair a Leadership Weakness or Improve a Strength

2. **Create a Robust Plan of Action** (Chapter 5)

    2.1   Commit to a Weekly Plan

    2.1   Determine How to Practice Leadership While You Work

    2.1   Get Specific

3. **Track Your Progress & Effort** (Chapter 6)

    3.1   Measure Progress and Effort to Grow Rapidly

    3.1   Reflect and Journal Successes and Failures

    3.1   Identify When to Switch Your Focus to New Skills

4. Anticipate Obstacles and Plan to Remove Them (Chapter 7)

    4.1   Identify Obstacles Before They Happen

    4.1   Attack Obstacles Head On

    4.1   Ask for Help

5. Seek Ongoing Feedback (Chapter 8)

    5.1   Ask Others to Help with Their Observations

    5.1   Adjust Your Plan Based on Feedback Trends

    5.1   Follow Through on What You Tell Others

These are the steps we will expand in the following chapters.

Chapter Four

Choose Wisely What to Improve

"Excellence is never an accident. It is always the result of high intention, sincere effort, and intelligent execution; it represents the wise choice of many alternatives – choice, not chance, determines your destiny."

Aristotle[17]

To randomly choose what you want to improve as a leader is the kiss of death for your leadership development. To rapidly develop your leadership ability, you must be diligent in choosing what to work on. Choosing wisely what to improve means:

1. Increase Self-awareness of Your Leadership Strengths and Weaknesses
2. Who Is Your Yardstick? (Who Do You Compare Yourself Against?)
3. Repair a Leadership Weakness or Improve a Strength

Increase Self-Awareness

When it comes to leadership, people often believe others see them as they see themselves. This is not accurate. Research from the leadership assessment company Zenger Folkman shows that our perceptions are only half as accurate as others. Therefore, it is not uncommon for a leader to have a blind spot; something he or she is unaware of that could be having a negative impact on their leadership ability. Usually, someone receiving feedback for the first time via a 360-degree assessment either rate their skills too harshly or think their skills are better than how others perceive them.

Receiving feedback about the current state of our leadership skills allows us to better understand others' perceptions. Without feedback, our personal awareness is based on our own perceptions, and we don't really know how others see us.

Are others' perceptions of us the "truth?" Or is your perception of yourself a more accurate assessment of "truth?" Reality is a combination of your self-awareness and the perceptions of others. Yet it is critical to know how our leadership lands on others. We must know that our followers' perceptions are critical to our leadership effectiveness, but it may not be the complete "truth."

Often, a leader is inspired to become better once he or she knows *how* the people they lead think of them. It might be the most important thing for your development as a leader. Your team's perceptions of your leadership effectiveness may not be the exact truth, but to them, it is their reality. If you don't know how your followers perceive you, how can you lead them effectively? It is a huge mistake to believe your self-perceptions are the truth.

> *"If you are leading a team and you turn around and no one is following you, you are just taking a walk."*
>
> **Phil McWaters**[18]

Let go of your self-perception and become curious about other people's perceptions of you. It often feels a little scary to search deeply for the things that others don't share with you. Some leaders know they are not the best leader and wonder if they have a blind spot.

A hospital Senior Director thought that his leadership style was exactly the style he needed to be successful. Throughout his career, he had made observations about what it took to be effective with the doctors and the administrators with whom he worked. He thought he needed to be tough-minded — to not to be rolled over by physicians and stay on top of administrators, following up with them. He justified his style of leadership based on his perception of what he thought would work best in the culture.

Unfortunately, he didn't know or seem to care what others thought about him and his "style." He was perceived as "arrogant, self-centered, uncaring, hard to work with, and rude." Of course, his peers, direct reports, and others didn't like working with him and complained to senior management and HR. Eventually, the organization had enough of his "style" and asked him to leave. This example is one of many that I've experienced that shows perception is reality. As a leader, you need to know what your followers' perceptions are if you want to improve your leadership.

If you can't see it, you can't change it. My wife was backing one of the kid's cars out of our driveway. We had two cars squeezed into the end of the driveway, and it was tricky. A basketball pole was next to the car she was backing out, and she didn't "see" it, hitting the basketball pole with the car. How did she not see it? She walked past it to get in the car. It stands 10 feet tall and is painted hunter green. But in her mind's eye, she did not have the awareness to see it as she backed out. I believe many leaders are the same way; they don't really see what effect their leadership is having on others. They tend to not see their own leadership impact, and therefore cannot improve it.

Who Is Your Yardstick? (Who Do You Compare Yourself Against?)

"Doug" wanted to get promoted and asked his boss what he could do to be better. His boss didn't have a specific suggestion. He told Doug to be patient, keep working hard, and deliver on his goals. In other words, just keep doing what you have been doing. Doug didn't feel satisfied that this advice would be enough to help him get the next job. He wondered about how good his skills really were. What if he was just average and not outstanding in any specific ways? He was concerned because he knew if he was not perceived as outstanding, a promotion would probably not be forthcoming.

What should Doug do? Just keep working harder? Attend a workshop on leadership? Read the latest leadership book and/or blogs? Listen to podcasts on leadership?

My clients know they need more than those things to improve. They desire to know what others think of them as a leader. Without this information, they could be wasting time, money, and energy trying to improve something that isn't going to help them become a better leader.

However, it is not enough for them to be able to just receive feedback, they want to receive results that can be compared with others who are highly skilled.

If your only comparison is with the other people in your company, you are probably missing something. Leadership effectiveness can be measured effectively. The best leaders know how their skills compare with those of other leaders outside of their company. How do you know how effective you are as a leader unless you have valid data that provides a comparison? Wouldn't it be great to know how you compare with leaders around the world? I work with clients who want to be world-class leaders and demand to have a comparison that shows them where they stand.

Good leadership is not good enough. Many leaders have set their sights too low. We need to compare ourselves with outstanding leaders. If you only compare against average leaders, you will miss an opportunity to become great.

Often, the impact of great versus good leadership is several multiples. To begin the process, you need to accurately understand your current level of leadership effectiveness.

Suggested Comparison Resource: 360-degree Assessments

I mentioned Zenger Folkman earlier, and their Extraordinary Leader 360-degree assessment[19] is excellent! It is based on two years of research and data that show what really differentiates poor, good, and great leadership. More than 100,000 leaders have taken the assessment. The size of the database allows someone who is serious about becoming an extraordinary leader the opportunity to have the best benchmark in the industry. When the scores for your leadership effectiveness are in the top 10% of 100,000 leaders around the world, you know for certain that your leadership is outstanding.

If you are unable to work with Zenger Folkman, I suggest you look for a leadership assessment that has a strong foundation of research. You should review the assessment report (ask for an example).

Your leadership development plan of action depends on your choice of a leadership competency. Not all leadership assessments are strength-based, and the assessment you choose should support that approach.

Are All Leadership Competencies the Same?

Through Zenger Folkman's assessment, leaders receive feedback on 19 "differentiating" leadership competencies. Their research suggests only these 19 competencies differentiate poor from good and extraordinary leadership. They have the research and statistical data to prove their assessment more accurately assesses leadership effectiveness than any other instrument in the market. There are many other reasons that you should consider using the Extraordinary Leader Assessment, but the main one is that you will be able to "choose wisely" what to improve.

I don't know of a better way to determine what an outstanding leader does than to use the 19 differentiating competencies. If you desire to become an extraordinary leader, and you want to be compared to leaders around the world to determine how effective you are, consider the Extraordinary Leader 360-degree Assessment. The Zenger Folkman 19 Differentiating Competencies are:

1. Displays High Integrity and Honesty
2. Technical/Professional Acumen
3. Solves Problems and Analyzes Issues

4. Innovates

5. Learning Agility

6. Drives for Results

7. Establishes Stretch Goals

8. Takes Initiative

9. Makes Decisions

10. Takes Risks

11. Communicates Powerfully and Prolifically

12. Inspires and Motivates Others to High Performance

13. Builds Relationships

14. Develops Others

15. Collaboration and Teamwork

16. Values Diversity

17. Develops Strategic Perspective

18. Champions Change

19. Customer and External Focus

Their research clearly shows that an extraordinary leader is highly proficient at 5 of the 19 competencies. They don't have to master all of them. Extraordinary leaders will have deficiencies; or said differently, they are not perfect. Just master five strengths!

More than any other step, this first step in the process derails people from effectively starting the process toward becoming a great leader. Most people try to do too much, or work on things that are not critical. If you try to be perfect and fix lower priority skills, you will waste a lot of time and energy. Even worse, you will not improve your overall effectiveness as a leader.

Repair a Leadership Weakness or Improve a Strength

Another big challenge people have in making the choice of what to work on is determining whether to work on improving a weakness or developing a strength. If you pick a weakness to improve, the chances are that, if you get better, that skill will only become average. It's almost impossible to make a weakness a strength.

Additionally, fixing a weakness is hard work because it is not fun; you often feel drained because you are not good at it. Therefore, it is hard to sustain any improvements. Some weaknesses just don't matter, but others are critical to the way the person does their work. You must be able to know the difference. Zenger Folkman's assessment does this for you.

If you don't have a critical weakness to improve, the key to the first step is accurately identifying a leadership strength that can leverage the way others perceive you as a leader. This is often a skill that improves other skills and helps leaders grow rapidly.

Performing Your Own Assessment

If you don't have the opportunity to use a 360-degree assessment to get feedback, you can start by creating a list of all the things you could do to improve your ability as a leader. Narrow the list down to three items that you think your company wants you to do, and ask yourself which ones you are the most excited to improve. Next, choose the one item from the three choices that is the most important to you.

When choosing what to work on, there is typically more than one right answer. So, you will need a way to determine which skill or competency to work on. First and foremost, it must be something important to the type of work you do every day. It must be a driver of success in your role. If you are a VP of finance, and you want to work on your ability to solve problems, I would ask if that is the highest and best use of your leadership. Surround yourself with good problem-solvers and work on a leadership ability that can galvanize the team.

Second, you need to choose something that is seen by your boss, yourself, and others as a critical skill in your role. What is the most important thing that would increase your ability to lead others successfully in your role? For 80% of people, they should choose something they are already good at, Or at least is an emerging strength. Unless you are brand-new to the role, the skill should be something you are passionate about and love doing.

The last criterion is passion, and more than any other factor, it is critical in determining the one thing you should work on. Do what is needed by the organization, do what you are good at, and do what you love. At the intersection of these three areas lies what you should work on.

As a leadership coach, I have met with many leaders who have previously received an in-depth feedback report from a 360-degree assessment or from a psychological assessment. These leaders were excited to learn more about themselves, but they were overwhelmed with the massive amount of information they received. Their attention was on all the things they 'should' work on. Trying to fix everything is a bad idea. And, in general, fixing things is usually a bad idea (unless it is a critical weakness for your job). I prefer a strengths-based approach that keeps people focused on developing one emerging strength at a time.

Reflection Questions

- Do you naturally want to fix a weakness or build on a strength?
- What leadership assessments are available to you? If none, how can you investigate using something with the accuracy and ability to help you choose wisely what to develop?

Chapter Five

Create a Robust Plan of Action

"A goal without a plan is just a wish."[20]

**— Antoine de Saint-Exupéry,
writer and pioneering aviator**

"By failing to prepare, you are preparing to fail."

**— Anonymous,
although popularly attributed to Benjamin Franklin,
Founding Father of the United States**

Dr. Prochaska and his fellow authors suggested "preparation" is a separate step in the process of changing for good. I agree wholeheartedly. Creating the plan of action might be the easiest, but most overlooked, step in the process. Prochaska writes: "Preparation takes you from the decisions you make in the contemplation stage to the specific steps you take to solve the problem during the action stage."[21] From my experience, the plan should include:

1. Commit to a Weekly Plan
2. Determine How to Practice Leadership While You Work
3. Get Specific

Commit to a Weekly Plan

For most people, committing to anything new is scary. We have tried to commit to things that we really wanted to do but failed. The only way to make significant change in our lives is to contemplate what our lives would be like after we accomplished the change. Additionally, we must see ourselves in action, doing the work and being successful along the way. Leadership development is the same thing.

Try creating a movie in your mind of you doing your work when you are leading. What are you doing? Presenting to your team? Speaking with great influence or listening with all your heart to another person? Helping someone solve a problem without telling them the answer? Creating new habits requires a vision and a commitment.

The commitment has to be big enough that when you are not making progress, or you haven't done what you said you planned to do, you find another gear and start over. Commitment is what drives us to pick ourselves up over and over. We commit to ourselves; and if we are smart, we commit to our teams and even our families to become the best leader possible.

When we commit ourselves to taking action and practicing different skills of leadership, we must also commit to a weekly plan. It starts with seeing that your leadership practice is as important as your meetings and all the to-do's that come your way. Commit to weekly practice.

Practice Leadership While You Work

One of the biggest mistakes people make is waiting for some free time to practice leadership skills. You will fail if you wait for the perfect time to practice. You will never not be too busy. To make a plan that tilts the scales toward success, you must integrate your weekly meeting schedule, to-do's, and leadership practice. An excellent plan has your leadership practices blocked out on your calendar, or at least at the top of your to-do list.

For example, if you are working on developing your skills at inspiring and motivating others, and you are specifically going to make better emotional connections with people, then your weekly plan needs to specifically identify when that is going to happen. During which meetings, with whom, and when do you plan to attempt to make better emotional connections? If you leave it to chance, you will not practice frequently enough.

Get Specific

Your plan of action should be detailed enough to keep you focused. You don't need a five-page plan, but something that should fit on one page, two-sided, and be so clear that you never have a doubt about what you are doing. The classic way to create a plan is to answer 'what,' 'when,' and 'how.' As you have read, passion is a driving factor in your motivation, so let's add to the list, "why."

Use your own format or come up with something that works for you. Some people are visual and enjoy using color and pictures. Others are bullet point people. Some need very little detail, and still others love to include a lot of detail. Do what works for you. Find a format that is motivational and inspires you.

If you are looking for a plan of action format, refer to the following example.

Leadership Development Action Plan Example

My Objective: to become an outstanding leader and have the influence and ability to help my team become the best they can. I want to help them feel successful and enjoy working together as a high performing team. I want to have a meaningful relationship with them in which they feel respected and trusted.

1. **My Leadership Strengths**
   - Can always be counted on to follow through on commitments (4.58)
   - Is careful to honor commitments and keep promises (4.42)
   - Is trusted by others to use good judgement when making decisions (4.42)

2. Potential Leadership Flaws

- Does an excellent job of marketing projects, programs or products (2.8)
- Brings to the group a high level of energy and enthusiasm (2.92)

3. My Passion and What the Organization Needs

- Collaboration and teamwork
- Develops others
- Inspires and motivates others to high performance
- Champions change

4. Potential Competencies to Strengthen

- Displays high integrity and honesty
- Solves problems and analyzes issues
- Drives for results
- Builds relationships
- Develops others
- Inspires and motivates others to high performance

5. My #1 Leadership Development Priority

- Displays high integrity and honesty

6. Ideas for Practice

- Meet with peers: first about findings, then regularly about other topics
- Meet with employees outside of direct reports
- Convey personal passion to the group
- Ask direct reports what inspires and motivates them

7. Implementation Actions

My Development Goal(s): Create positive relationships with my peers

Specific Actions I Will Take: meet with at least two peers-no specific agenda. If I can positively help with/affect the big issues we are dealing with I think that will go a long way in building trust. Also meet with non-direct reports (the tendon team would be the best because they are offsite, and I rarely see/speak with them)

Date by Which I Will Complete the Goal: 2/8/19

Ways to Keep my Focus on This Goal: Schedule it in Outlook

Potential Barriers/Obstacles: Peers travel schedule, meetings, literally daily issues that "pop up" and need immediate attention, getting distracted and not practicing

How to Overcome Them: Phone calls, schedule in Outlook (so a new meeting can't be booked), have team text me for urgent issues instead of expecting an immediate email response

Support/Resources I May Need: Mentor support for the larger issue=how to handle certain situations.

If your goal is to become an outstanding leader in one year, you will need to practice every week. This is possible only if you plan your leadership practice. The more practice the better. For instance, if you only "inspire and motivate" one time per week versus two or three times, you won't grow and learn as fast as you can.

Break down your one-year development process into 52 weekly projects. Each week, start with a specific idea of what you are going to do. At the end of the week, take 30 minutes and evaluate the progress that week. Maybe you didn't do what you planned on doing, but if you assess the lack of progress at the end of the week, you can at least reset your plan for the next week. That way, you should never lose more than a week from inactivity. You will want to maximize your learning. As I said before, the more you practice, the better the chance you have of getting better.

Specific Plans Only Work When Revised Frequently

Most important is to know the plan you create is never final; it is just the current draft from which you are working. Your plan should be flexible enough to be revised. Fluid planning, not fixed. Determine what works to keep you focused and working your plan as well as you can. When the plan is not serving you, change it. Be willing to try something and know that failure brings great learning. Plans that are static tend to fail.

Keep your practice ideas fresh and exciting. Look for better and more challenging ways to practice the skill you are trying to perfect before you move on to another skill or competency. Only after you have consistently practiced for a few months and received positive feedback, can you start working on a new skill or competency.

After a few months of consistent deep practice, when the new skill is feeling like a habit, you may ask yourself if you should move on to another skill. Don't move on to another skill or competency unless you have exhausted all the levels of practice. Maybe you have been able to make an emotional connection with your direct reports, but you have not even tried to do it with your boss. You don't even know where to begin, and it scares you to death. That would be a good indicator that you are not finished practicing this important skill. If there are things that will push you out of your comfort zone, don't jump to the next skill. Wait until you have exhausted all the practice opportunities for the skill you are working on before jumping to the next leadership skill.

Chapter Six

Track Your Progress & Effort

"You don't make progress by standing on the sidelines, whimpering and complaining. You make progress by implementing ideas."

Shirley Chisholm[22]

Perhaps it seems elementary that you would track your progress and effort as you work toward becoming an excellent leader. However, my experience has shown that almost no one does this on their own. I imagine that since the goal is not a tangible goal, such as the creation of a business result, it might not get tracked. It is very rare that a developing leader would:

1. Measure Progress and Effort to Grow Rapidly
2. Reflect and Journal Successes and Failures
3. Identify When to Switch Your Focus to New Skills

Measure Progress and Effort

Leaders who make the most progress in developing their leadership ability manage it like any other project. A plan must be established; but without tracking progress against the plan, you will never know if progress is being made. If you were running a big project for your company, and the CEO wanted to know the project's status, you would be embarrassed if you couldn't supply an answer. It's our project, and we need to be able to indicate whether or not we are making progress.

I'm amazed at people who are discouraged at their rate of progress, but don't assess their effort. So, when I work with a client, I ask them to assess their effort as well as their progress. Low effort always yields slow progress. To keep yourself accountable to your plan, assessing your effort level has a lot to do with creating developmental momentum.

When you are experiencing developmental momentum, you enjoy every aspect of your leadership development process. You look forward to trying new things; and when you do, you get a little jolt because you did something different. You love reflecting on what you did and what you learned. Every time you experience an 'ah-ha,' some dopamine is released in your brain and you can't wait to learn something new again. You consistently ask others for feedback because every time you do, a new insight is gained.

"Good intentions pave the way to hell."

— Anonymous

If you want incredible results in your development process, learn to consistently assess your effort. When you are tracking your progress, you must also ask yourself if you are putting in your best effort. If you are not 100% accountable to the effort you give your plan, you will probably be disappointed in the result. You need to make sure that your effort and commitment stay strong. Everyone starts with a high level of commitment, but it easily gets diminished with other priorities that interfere with development. Good intentions are not enough.

However, failing to give your development practice as much effort as you had planned will occasionally happen. That's not a big problem, unless one poor week of effort turns into two weeks, and then a month. Very few people ever start over after a month of inactivity. It is the most frequent reason for failure in leadership development. Because leadership development takes place over the course of months and years, we need "accountability practices," such as regularly (at least monthly) measuring our progress and effort.

A wonderful friend once said to me, "You need to hold me accountable!" I shot back to him that I would not hold him accountable, but that he needed to hold himself accountable, and I would be willing to help him do that. It does help to have a person who will enable your accountability at a high level. You need to keep yourself focused on your development plan, and that means you should track your leadership skills practice. Be accountable to yourself and your plan.

The holy grail of accountability is committing to measuring your leadership effectiveness and your progress in developing your leadership skills and competencies. At the end of the development process, quantitatively measure progress by using the same assessment tool with which you started the process. There is no wiggle room for a leader when they know their leadership effectiveness will be evaluated at the end of the process.

It is not a foregone conclusion that your reassessment will show progress unless your effort during the development process was consistent and at a reasonable level. This is why I keep suggesting that practicing the most highly leverageable skills every week and reflecting on what you learned is the heavy lifting of leadership development. Doing the work consistently with the proper evaluation creates results.

Reflecting & Journaling

A great way to do this is on Saturday morning with a cup of coffee. Pull out your leadership journal and reflect on how well you performed leadership actions in the past week. Break down each meeting, noting what worked and what didn't. You will see the mistakes and determine ways to improve – don't judge them as bad or wrong. Be curious. Curiosity is the energy of a great learner. Your reflection will give you insights and inspiration to continue developing yourself. Commit to reflecting on your progress every week.

Journaling is sometimes confused with writing in a diary. They are not even remotely the same. Your journal is your learning friend that is always there to challenge you to think deeply. It is a tool to help you learn how to ask yourself challenging questions and search within yourself for the answer. The harder the question, the better your insights. Sometimes I ask a tough question and just sit and think. As I reflect, I force my brain into deep reflection, which helps to create mastery.

A great way to do this is to think back over the past week and run the leadership practices you had in your mind; 'roll the tape.' Just like a sports team reviews their performances on video, play the video in your mind. See yourself in action, what you did, what they did, and the outcome. Being able to view yourself as you practice your leadership enables your success at becoming an outstanding leader. It is important to notice your successes and failures, as both provide meaningful insights on how to perform as a leader.

It only takes 20-30 minutes a week to use journaling to keep yourself accountable to your leadership development plan, and it can be done by answering seven questions: (A form for your use is in the appendix)

1. What did I plan to do this week?
2. What did I do? Was my effort as good as it could be?
3. What worked that I want to keep doing?
4. What didn't work? What should I do differently the next time I practice this skill?
5. What did I learn?
6. What do I plan to do next week?
7. Where do I need help? (information, ideas, insights, feedback etc.)

When to Switch to the Next Skill or Competency

When you thoroughly practice your leadership skills and competencies, you will notice through your weekly reflection that you are not learning as much as before after you practiced a skill. This is the first sign that it is time to move on to the next skill or competency. However, the concern I share with most of my clients is that they should not work on too many things at once. Your focus on a singular competency and the behaviors that support that competency will yield high results. If you jump around week to week to different leadership actions, you can get overwhelmed, and your learning may not result in new habits.

Watch Out: Comfort Zones & Habits

One idea about deep practice that I have not mentioned yet is the importance of pushing yourself out of your comfort zone. Humans are psychologically wired to seek comfort and to stay within their comfort zone. We don't naturally seek to be uncomfortable; therefore, to accomplish the most from our deep practice, it is important to make sure we don't allow ourselves to skip the practice that makes us uncomfortable.

This is a good description of what happens in our brains by "KwikLearning.com:"

"Our brains are busy – At any given moment, your brain is performing countless functions simultaneously. It is home to more than 100 billion cells that are constantly forming different neural pathways for processing different kinds of information. It needs a huge amount of energy for doing all of that; in fact, the brain alone hogs the lion's share of your body's energy reserve."

"We are designed to conserve energy – Because our brain needs so much energy just to function, we have evolved to seek out ways to perform any given actions using the least amount of energy possible. Falling into habits and following the same neural pathways all the time help conserve energy, so our brain is automatically predisposed to the comfort zone."

"Our brain wants to keep us safe – Humans are evolved for survival, and the best way to do that is to avoid danger. Our brain's threat-response system works according to that design. Any new thing awakes our primal fear of the unknown. The comfort zone is basically our survival instinct working overtime, telling you to stay away from potentially threatening situations, and walking the tried and tested road."[23]

For example, if I want to be a better listener, I might say to myself that I am going to stop interrupting people. When I am consciously aware of how I am or am not doing it, I can temporarily change. But as soon as I take my consciousness off of listening, I fall back into my old habit. My comfort is clearly to do what I have always done. It's easier, and my brain tells me that changing something like this is going to be so difficult that it won't be worth it.

"You can't do it; you have never been a good listener. Why try?"

"You can't teach old dogs new tricks."

"Just stop working on this and do something more important."

Your comfort zone can expand with practice and consciousness. It does not have control of you, but combined with the power of your existing habits, it can make changing your behavior extremely difficult.

"Old habits are strong and jealous"

—Dorothea Brande[24]

One of the reasons "practice" is so necessary is that you might have an old habit that needs to be replaced with a new habit. It has been said by those who have studied habits and the brain that, "you never get rid of habits; you just replace them with stronger habits." New habits are weak and need to be reinforced. If you don't do something multiple times with some level of success, a new habit will be unlikely to take root. Your goal should be to practice and notice how the new skill or practice worked every time you use it.

For instance; active listening is a skill of outstanding leaders. If you are practicing listening actively, you might notice that you connect better with others, enabling them to be heard. The observation of something working helps tremendously to solidify your commitment to continuing to listen actively. Success begets success.

In the end, your success or failure at becoming an extraordinary leader will be due to how well you create new habits. It all comes down to behavior change. Frequent practice of the same skills and competencies can yield tremendous new habits, because of the new neural pathways that are being created in our brain each time we practice these new behaviors.

The best book I have ever read on behavior change is James Clear's book called *Atomic Habits – An Easy and Proven Way to Build Good Habits and Break Bad Ones*.[25] I don't want to summarize his book here. The book is chocked full of practical suggestions that create "tiny changes, remarkable results." I have used his idea of "habit stacking" to create a new habit. I strongly suggest reading the book and checking out his website: james-clear.com.

Chapter Seven

Anticipate Obstacles

"Obstacles don't have to stop you. If you run into a wall, don't turn around and give up. Figure out how to climb it, go through it, or work around it."

Michael Jordan[26]

In this chapter, I will identify the key obstacles that you will experience in your leadership development, and provide some suggestions about how to remove them. Hopefully, with this information, you will be able to identify obstacles before they happen; and because you are prepared, attack them head on. However, regarding the third sub-step, you will need to determine when to "ask for help."

- Identify Obstacles Before They Happen
- Attack Obstacles Head On
- Ask for Help

Identify Obstacles Before They Happen

People with good intentions fail all the time. Whether it is someone who wants to become a better leader or someone who wants to lose weight or stop smoking, it is a difficult challenge.

"Most diets fail, and MOST will regain their lost weight in one to five years."

**— Long Term Diet Failure,
The Council on Size and Weight Discrimination.**[27]

Like a new diet, you will face many obstacles as you attempt to develop your leadership skills. I'll address obstacles and how to overcome them in this chapter.

When we declare to ourselves and others that we are going to become an outstanding leader, we are declaring that we will change our behaviors. What gets in the way of most behavioral change? We have met the enemy—and it is us. We are the greatest obstacle to becoming outstanding leaders. It is always our habits, comfort zones, limiting beliefs, victim thinking, lack of follow-through, lack of planning, lack of discipline, lack of measurement, and inability to ask for help. Most of us don't have experience at changing ourselves. We can do it, but we need help.

Marshall Goldsmith was named one of the five most respected executive coaches by Forbes and a top-10 "executive educator" by *The Wall Street Journal*. In his book, *What Got You Here, Won't Get You There*,[28] he affirms that we need to understand the power of making small changes consistently over time, in order to make the biggest changes in ourselves. He hired someone to call him at 10 o'clock every night and ask him some accountability questions: "Did you do your best at . . . asking curious questions, listening to others without interrupting, expressing love and gratitude?"

Marshall's goal is to do these things every day. He knows if they are not tracked, obstacles will get in the way of doing them. He is accountable to report daily on the small habits he values and wants to create. Obstacles will show up in his analysis, as he reviews the "data" and trends. Do you have a tracking mechanism that can identify when an obstacle is preventing you from making the progress you desire?

Anticipating the Need for Help

Who helps you be accountable? I wrote earlier that you need to hold yourself accountable; but let me also say that this seems to be the hardest part of developing yourself into an outstanding leader.

What options do you have? You could ask your spouse to follow up with you, but the potential friction that might arise makes the spouse my least favorite choice. You could ask a friend who knows you well and is aware of your tendencies. Not all friends will be tough enough or follow up as often as you might need, but other friends might be excellent. You could also ask a peer at work to help you. If the peer cares deeply about you and your success, they might be outstanding. However, they must be the kind of person who will not listen to excuses and will help you face your failures.

Coaches are marvelous sources of wisdom and can provide deeper insights and learning by asking the tough questions. Coaching meetings keep you on track because you don't want to disappoint someone else. Coaches provide structure, process, tracking, support, encouragement, and a pathway to excel at behavioral development.

Obstacles can be identified; and if they can be identified, they can be minimized. When I ask people which obstacles they might be challenged with during their leadership development process, they don't have a hard time listing what they expect to face. Here's the 'short' list of potential obstacles:

- Lack of time
- Loss of focus
- Lack of energy
- Not tracking progress
- Expecting it to happen faster
- Getting discouraged
- Not receiving feedback
- Trying to work on too many things at once

- Not asking for help
- Doing things that don't make a difference

I believe we can list most of our obstacles, and we can determine ways to overcome them. A good leadership development plan includes a list of obstacles and the ways you will work around them. A better plan is to include someone like a coach to keep you focused on your plan, minimize the length of time you are not making progress, and help you get past obstacles quicker.

Attack Obstacles Head On

A big part of your plan should be a section that outlines specific personal obstacles and what you will do about them. Don't be shy! The more the better. Obstacles are an interference to your progress; and just like any interference, if you acknowledge it, you take its power away. "Power" is having a plan to use when you notice the obstacle. Your success as a leader is important, and becoming outstanding is a demanding process. You can minimize the chance of failing if you determine in advance what will derail you.

To get you started planning for obstacles, let's take a few of the most prevalent obstacles and start to plan for them. Note, these ideas may not resonate with you, but they will start you thinking about ideas that will work for you.

Lack of Time

This is probably the number one mentioned obstacle. I always ask people who bring it up whether they think it is a real obstacle or not. Most leaders think about it for a while and then tell me it's more of an excuse. However, it is such a powerful distraction that it can get in the way. In my experience, the best way to overcome a lack of time is to block out time on your calendar to do leadership practice and reflection. If it is not on your calendar, it probably won't happen on its own. Make sure at the beginning of every week, you have a plan to use your new leadership skills and when you are going to do your reflection.

Lack of Progress

This is a combination of a few items and can be confusing for someone who may be experiencing it, because there are multiple root causes for it: not practicing enough, not reflecting on what each practice is teaching, not tracking effort, and not asking others for additional feedback. To create more progress, start with ensuring you are working on developing a competency that the company needs and one that you are passionate about. And then go down the gut check list of questions:

1. How many times did you practice this past week and past month?
2. Are you giving your plan as much effort as you can? If not, how do you take it to the next level?
3. Do you have at least one insight about what you have learned by reflecting on what you did? Are you journaling every week?
4. Do you have an idea of how others perceive your progress and what leadership actions are changing/improving? If not, who can you ask for specific feedback?
5. Are you working on the right thing? Are you trying to improve something with a low degree of importance? Or are you possibly working on too many things?

Lack of Progress in Changing a Habit

The process of personal change can be difficult for those who have never before challenged themselves to change something significant. When working to reduce the negative impact from a bad habit, it requires a great plan to build stronger habits around it. Until you can "rely" on the new habit(s) unconsciously, it will not feel natural. Making progress can be associated with the strength of your new habits.

If, for instance, you have always interrupted people and you are trying not to interrupt others, you need other habits:

- Act as if your job is to summarize or paraphrase what they just said
- Ask another question based on what they just told you
- Make sure you make eye contact
- Let silence occur after the other person is done talking

These other habits must become strong enough to overcome the power of the habit of interrupting. Focus on establishing confidence by practicing one of these behaviors.

Expecting it to Happen Faster, and Getting Discouraged When It Doesn't

If we don't track our progress, and things don't change quickly, doubt creeps in and we start to think that maybe the process is not going to work for us. Discouragement sets in and we become so frustrated that we quit. This is a normal emotional obstacle that can completely stop the process of personal change.

The antidote for this obstacle is to do two things. First, identify that this is a multi-month process, and that after three months of consistently practicing, reflecting, and measuring progress & effort, you will start to see some significant changes. Change will begin as early as the first month, and some big improvements will be noticed in the first 90-days; but significant and lasting changes might take six months. So, establishing a realistic expectation is very important.

Second, being committed to doing the work of leadership development is critical. What that means is practicing leadership acts, noticing, and reflecting about the impact. But it also means accurately assessing your progress and effort every week. When you look for progress and effort weekly, you will find ways to improve both. Discouragement does not set in when you are always thinking about how to improve your progress and effort.

Trying to Work on Too Many Things at Once, or Doing Things That Don't Make a Difference

This one is simple: don't choose more than one competency to work on at a time! Don't be tempted. If you have chosen a strength to work on, you will need 2-3 ways to practice that strength (ideally in a cross-training way). Additionally, the one thing that you choose to work on needs to be important to your work and your role. If you choose something that your boss and others don't think is the most important thing for you to be doing, their perception of you becoming a better leader may not change. So, choose the one competency that if done with excellence will help your team and your organization the most.

Ask for Help

Your development is your plan. You own it; but if it is 'private,' something that you try to do alone, you will probably fail. I call this going down into your private rabbit hole. Leadership is not a private act — it must be done with and for others. So, your leadership development plan needs to include others.

You can and should ask for people's feedback throughout the process. Their insights matter, and can help you see things that you don't see on your own. You will need to hear from others that they see progress, to help you feel good, and to know that you are going in the right direction.

Asking for help means reaching out to your boss or others who have a special skill or ability, and asking them about what they do and how they do it. Learning from others about how they do something well is a great idea, if you want to grow your leadership skills. Learn from the best to become the best. Ask someone who does what you want to do well, how they do it and how they learned how to do it well.

Beware of Keeping Your Leadership Development Private

If you go 'private' with your development, meaning that no one knows you are working on becoming an outstanding leader, you will probably not get the results you desire. A better option is to make a public announcement that you are going to work on becoming an outstanding leader, and you will need your team's help to get there. Additionally, if you help people understand that you are doing it for the team's benefit, it helps get their buy-in to support the plan. The plan is that they will provide feedback during the process, so you know what is working and what is not working from their perspective.

Because leadership effectiveness is in the eye of the beholder, we need to ask our followers if they see anything different. If we don't ask those who will be giving us the final feedback how we are doing along the way, they might not have any idea that we are working on a skill; therefore, their perception of our effectiveness may not change.

I taught leadership classes with a guy who received feedback that he was not training his employees enough. It upset him because he thought he was always training people. His idea of training was not a classroom-based experience, but one that happens in one-on-one meetings. Thus, for the next several months, every time one of his team members came to his office for a meeting, he would pull out a name plate that had the word "training" on it. He would tell them that part of the meeting was for their training purposes. As a result, his direct report's perception changed. The next time he asked for feedback, he received good scores for training employees. Did he change his behavior? Yes and no – he helped people see more clearly what he was already doing.

This story makes me smile. It may not give you the best way to increase your leadership effectiveness, but it does capture the idea that development must not be a private affair. We need to seek feedback from our team at least once a quarter. Make sure you incorporate others' feedback into your development plan.

Chapter Eight

Seek Ongoing Feedback

*"We all need people who will give us feedback.
That's how we improve."*

Bill Gates[29]

"Feedback is the breakfast of champions."

Ken Blanchard[30]

The fifth step is to seek ongoing feedback. It is the hardest of the five steps to do. I don't know exactly why, but I suspect that we all want to look like we have our act together. We want to be perceived as competent, and when we ask others for feedback, we don't feel like we know everything we 'should' know. If our organizations were good at learning, we would feel differently about asking for information that could help us learn. But because of our pride and ego, we struggle with asking others for their feedback. It is not a good idea to develop yourself for a year or longer without getting additional feedback along the way.

- Ask Others to Help with Their Observations
- Adjust Your Plan Based on Feedback Trends
- Follow Through on What You Tell Others

Ask Others to Help with Their Observations

From the researchers at Zenger Folkman, we know that leaders who have an overall leadership effectiveness score at the 90th percentile or higher are people who give feedback and ask for feedback frequently. Therefore, we know it is a highly leverageable leadership act to ask for feedback.

A good way to do this is to start the process by thanking the people who gave you feedback in the initial 360-degree assessment, telling them what you learned, and what you plan to do. At that time, you can ask them for feedback throughout the process. If you enroll them at the start of the process, it won't seem weird to them if you ask them for additional feedback every three months. This is called making a "declaration," and it can help people see you as a leader.

I don't think you need more than three or four people to give you additional feedback. Ideally, if your boss has an objective view of your leadership, he or she should be one of the feedback providers. The right people can help you see things that you don't see on your own.

I suggest giving your feedback providers some questions to think about a week before you meet with them, to help them know what questions you are going to ask. You could start with something like, "Compared to three months ago, have you noticed any changes in my leadership? If so, what things have you noticed?" I also suggest asking specifically about the leadership skills and competencies you are trying to change. For instance, "What things have I done to inspire and motivate you more in the last 90 days?"

Zenger Folkman provides a "pulse assessment," so their clients can receive feedback through an electronic assessment and get anonymous feedback in a report. Try to find an assessment company that also provides pulse surveys and reassessments. If that is not available, you could have someone collect the information for you. I have conducted interviews and summarized the key findings in an anonymous report to validate a leader's progress and things they could do differently.

Adjust Your Plan Based on Feedback Trends

When you get feedback, you will either feel good that you are going in the right direction or know you need to change direction. If you don't know how others (especially those you lead) perceive your improvement as a leader, there may be a surprise for you when you complete your reassessment at the end of the development process. Everyone would like to know if their hard work is paying off, and if not, what else they could do to become a better leader.

Follow Through on What You Tell Others

Your plan of action should be fluid enough to allow for revisions as you receive feedback, or when you think it needs to change based on your assessment. Make sure you don't ignore others' feedback – act on what you were told; follow through. One of the best leadership actions is to ask for feedback and be curious about what you are being told. But even more important is to follow through on what you were told. That is the true mark of an outstanding leader.

Reflection

If you have made it this far into the book, I am sure you are highly motivated to initiate the process of developing yourself into an outstanding leader. You may be experiencing a little anxiety. The best way to prepare is by creating a project plan for the actions you need to take. You can start by answering these questions:

1. What's your motivation, the reason you want to do this?
2. How are you going to get feedback about your skills - what assessment tool can you access?
3. Who can help you understand the data from the assessment tool and guide you in creating an effective action plan?
4. How will you practice your new leadership skills?

5. How will you measure your progress and effort?

6. How will you be accountable?

7. Who will give you feedback throughout the process?

8. Who will help you understand why you do what you do, and how you can change your tendency to not lead effectively?

9. Who will help you see what you don't see?

10. How will you practice deeply and incorporate learning through reflective journaling?

Conclusion

Over the course of my career, I have worked for great bosses and lousy bosses. I thought I could be independent of their positive and negative effects. I was wrong. I was strongly influenced by both. I think we all desire to work for a great leader. I stopped working for my great leader over 25 years ago, but I still can remember the impact that person had on my life, and the organization. When you experience the difference between great and poor leadership, you don't need to read a book on leadership. You know what it feels like, and you know what it looks like. Followers know the difference, that's why 360-degree assessments are valuable.

If we all know the difference, why are there not more outstanding leaders? I think it's because we don't have enough good examples, our cultures push us in the wrong direction, and we don't have effective leadership development processes to help us. I have struggled in my own career to lead well, and from years of connecting the dots on my own, I may have finished my corporate career as someone who others 'enjoyed' working for. Best Boss Ever – I'm not sure if I made it that far, but I think I got close. My 360-degree assessment showed it, and the relationships I had supported it.

My wish for you, is that you can get there faster than my contemporaries and me. I hope that you will make it a priority to lead others in extraordinary ways. And I pray that the difference you make in the world will make a bigger impact than you could have ever hoped. My dream is that by giving you the process and the knowledge (born from many others' failures) to develop yourself, that you will be able to be the *Best Boss Ever*.

Appendix

1. The 26-week plan (7 questions)
2. Top 50 Outstanding Leadership Actions
3. Stages of Change Self-Assessment
4. Leadership Development Plan

Visit donfrericks.com to access the BBE Resources page

Leadership Articles

For your further reading, I have created a series of articles to provide you specific insights about the skills and abilities that great leaders have. Please go to my website, donfrericks.com, to read the articles in their entirety. The following is a brief description of each article.

Why Bad Leadership Is So Bad

From my experience, I believe that bad leaders learn from other bad leaders. They don't always know the extent to which their negative leadership reaches. They think this style of leadership works, and, as long as it works, they will continue to use it. They usually lack emotional intelligence and are missing key "EQ" competencies.

One common form of bad leadership is often called out as "micromanagement."

Do you have a proclivity to closely manage your people so that they don't make a big mistake, and/or do you try to stay informed of everything they are doing so you know if they are productive? Do you know how your team would answer these questions? Taken to extremes, these tendencies can become serious fatal flaws that minimize leadership effectiveness.

What's the Difference Between Managing and Leading?

Is management and leadership the same thing? Is management a bad thing? Can I become a great leader if I am stuck in a situation that requires a lot of managing? Is someone considered a leader because of their title?

No, managing and leading are not the same thing. Managing is about the day-to-day coordination of resources to accomplish goals. Leading is about the people, and includes inspiring, motivating, engaging, enrolling, and empowering people to accomplish a mission and vision. We manage things and lead people.

Employee Disengagement Flows from Poor Leadership

Christine Porath is an associate professor at the McDonough School of Business at Georgetown University, and she has polled tens of thousands of workers worldwide about how they are treated at work.

She writes: *"Leadership is crucial. In my research, the number-one attribute that garnered commitment and engagement from employees was respect from their leaders. In fact, no other leadership behavior had a greater effect on employees across the outcomes measured. Being treated with respect was more important to employees than recognition and appreciation, communicating an inspiring vision, providing useful feedback, or even providing opportunities for learning, growth, and development."*

Is Motivation Your Big Obstacle?

What's your motivation to be an outstanding leader? Why do you want to be the best boss ever? Knowing the answer to these questions is important. There are two ways to find the answer; contemplation or reacting to an emergency; which is often a 'wake-up' call – something so abrupt it makes us take stock of ourselves and answer the hard questions.

Improving leadership effectiveness starts with leading yourself better. If you can't lead yourself effectively, you can't lead others. Starting the process without deeply contemplating how your life will be better when you become an outstanding leader is an error. You will need tremendous motivation to begin the process of developing your leadership ability. Start by contemplating what your life will be like when you can lead yourself and others with excellence.

Knowledge is Power

Emerging outstanding leaders must be able to identify the things they do to hold themselves back and/or what they do to be more effective. My experience shows that leaders who regularly use deep practice accelerate their development faster than others. It is a process of reflection and journaling.

Journaling helps us contemplate. To move ourselves from precontemplation to contemplation, reflect and think about what could happen in the future.

Motivation and Mindsets

In your planning stage, it is important to assess your mindset. I suggest looking inward to see if your passion to become an outstanding leader is built on a strong and deep foundation. You will need to know your 'why' and your motivation will be tested as you develop your skills as a leader. It will happen, your skills will become better, and others will perceive you as a great leader.

"The passion for stretching yourself and sticking to it, even (or especially) when it is not going well, is the hallmark of the growth mindset. It leads to a desire to learn, and therefore, a tendency to embrace challenges, persist in the face of setbacks, see effort as the path to mastery, learn from criticism, and find lessons and inspiration in the success of others." — Carol Dweck

Don Frericks –
Executive Leadership Coach

After many years of working in the corporate world and as an executive coach, Don Frericks has witnessed firsthand the positive and negative effect leaders can have on their teams. His experience comes from 25 years in leadership roles within companies such as Cintas, Cincinnati Bell, and the US Bank. Don himself knows the exhilaration of working with a great leader, and the unrelenting despair of working under a bad leader. This experience on both sides of the corporate continuum formed the foundation of Don's leadership observations.

Because he has experienced both sides, Don loves to help leaders identify the most impactful and necessary change in their leadership, and bring it to pass. His technique for focusing on the most leverageable change brings immediate results that can be felt and seen by both small and large organizations. He finds great fulfillment in working closely with top executives to shape them into better leaders.

For more than seven years, Don has served as a consultant who focuses on organizational improvement and executive coaching with companies such as Procter & Gamble, LexisNexis, Reynolds & Reynolds, Brown Forman, Humana, and many others. His practical business background and extensive experiences as an executive coach enable Don to appreciate the complexities of leading people through significant organizational change.

As a thank you for reading my book, I would love to share with you a complimentary copy of my white paper that I referenced throughout this book:

"HOW WE BECAME LEADERS

THEMES FROM 22 STORIES ABOUT THE JOURNEY TO LEADERSHIP AND WHAT IT MEANS FOR FUTURE LEADERS"

You may download it from my website:
www.donfrericks.com

Ready to Up Your Game? Reach out for a complimentary consultation to develop your leadership development plan don@donfrericks.com.

I thrive on success stories, please tell me yours!
Send me your story and I'll share it with everyone else in my network to give them hope and inspiration.

Notes

[1] Jack Zenger and Joe Folkman, *The Extraordinary Leader* (New York, New York: McGraw-Hill Companies, 2002, 2009), Page 29.

[2] Ibid.

[3] Anthony J. Reilly & Tim Boone, *Improving Leadership Effectiveness: The Leader Match Concept.* (Fred E. Fiedler and Martin M. Chemers with Linda Mahar, New York: John Wiley, 1976. Group & Organization Studies 2-2), Pages 254-255. https://doi.org/10.1177/105960117700200218

[4] Adam Hickman and Jeremy Pietrocini, (2019, May 8). *How to Help Your Managers Build Out, Not Burn Out.* Retrieved January 1, 2020, from https://www.gallup.com/workplace/249140/inspire-management-breakthrough-not-breakdown.aspx.

[5] Quoting Mattson Newell (2016, June 10) *What You Can Learn from Vince Lombardi's Timeless Leadership Wisdom.* Retrieved February 11, 2020 from https://www.partnersinleadership.com/insights-publications/can-learn-vince-lombardis-timeless-leadership-wisdom/.

[6] James Prochaska, John C. Norcross, and Carlo C. DiClemente, *Changing for Good: A Revolutionary Six-Stage Program for Overcoming Bad Habits and Moving Your Life Positively Forward* (New York, New York: Quill, 1994), Page 58.

[7] Ibid. Page 59.

[8] Ibid. Page 74.

[9] Ibid. Page 89.

[10] Mike Myatt, (2012, December 19). *The #1 Reason Leadership Development Fails.* Retrieved January 26, 2020, from https://www.forbes.com/sites/mikemyatt/2012/12/19/the-1-reason-leadership-development-fails/#64818dbc6522.

[11] Jeff Schwartz, Uda Bohdal-Spiegelhoff, Michael Gretczko, and Nathan Sloan, *Global Human Capital Trends 2016* (New York, New York: Deloitte University Press, 2016), Page 5. Retrieved January 26, 2020, from https://www2.deloitte.

com/content/dam/Deloitte/global/Documents/HumanCapital/gx-dup-global-human-capital-trends-2016.pdf.

12 Myatt, Ibid.

13 *Size of the Training Industry* (2019, April 23). Retrieved February 13, 2020, from https://trainingindustry.com/wiki/outsourcing/size-of-training-industry/.

14 Malcom Gladwell, *Outliers: The Story of Success* (New York, New York: Back Bay Books, 2011).

15 Janet Clarey, *Creating an Agile Learning Culture* (New York, New York: Deloitte University Press, 2013), Page 13. Retrieved January 27, 2020, from https://www.ebscohost.com/uploads/_temp/031913_Clarey_BbD_EBSCO.pdf.

16 Jack Zenger and Joe Folkman, (2009, June). *Ten Fatal Flaws that Derail Leaders.* Retrieved January 27, 2020, from https://hbr.org/2009/06/ten-fatal-flaws-that-derail-leaders.

17 *The Complete Works of Aristotle: The Revised Oxford Translation.* Ed. Jonathan Barnes, 2 vols. (Princeton, NJ: Princeton Univ. Press, 1984).

18 Heard by the author during a live session by Phil McWaters at Proctor &Gamble's 'Band 4 College,' September, 2019.

19 Joe Folkman, (2019, August). *Extraordinary Leader 360-Degree Survey.* Retrieved February 8, 2020, from https://zengerfolkman.com/wp-content/uploads/2019/08/EL360Survey_WP-2019.pdf.

20 Antoine de Saint-Exupéry, *Airman's Odyssey: A Trilogy Comprising Wind, Sand and Stars, Night Flight [and] Flight to Arras* (San Diego, California: Harcourt, Brace & World, 1965).

21 Prochaska, Norcross, and DiClemente, Ibid. Page 146.

22 As quoted in *The Journal of Social Work Education*, Volume 44 (Council on Social Work Education, Northwestern University, 2008), Page 33.

23 *'Comfort Zone' Can Put Your Brain to Sleep. Here's How to Break Out of It!* (2019, February 25). By KwikLearning.com. Accessed February 8, 2020, from https://kwiklearning.com/kwik-tips/comfort-zone-can-put-your-brain-to-sleep-heres-how-to-break-out-of-it/.

24 Dorothea Brande, *Dorothea Brande's Wake Up and Live! Collection* (Lulu Press, Inc., 2017), Page 129.

25 James Clear, *Atomic Habits – An Easy and Proven Way to Build Good Habits and Break Bad Ones* (New York, New York: Avery-Penguin Random House, 2018).

26 As quoted in Dr. Kenneth Augustus Walker, *Pits and Palaces: Overcoming Every Obstacle in Your Life* (Bloomington, Indiana: Trafford Publishing, 2014), Page 111.

[27] Summary of study results, *Long Term Diet Failure*, (2020, January 30). Council on Size and Weight Discrimination. Accessed February 8, 2020, from http://cswd.org/long-term-diet-failure.

[28] Marshall Goldsmith, *What Got You Here, Won't Get You There* (London, England: Profile Books, 2010).

[29] Bill Gates, *Teachers Need Real Feedback* (TED Conferences, LLC, 2013). Accessed on February 8, 2020, from https://www.ted.com/talks/bill_gates_teachers_need_real_feedback/transcript.

[30] Quoting Rick Tate, Ken Blanchard, (2009, August 17). *Feedback is the Breakfast of Champions*. Retrieved February 8, 2020, from https://www.kenblanchardbooks.com/feedback-is-the-breakfast-of-champions/.